A LEVEL FOR EVERY READER

This book is a part of an exciting four-level reading series to support children in developing the habit of reading widely for both pleasure and information. Each book is designed to develop a child's reading skills, fluency, grammar awareness, and comprehension in order to build confidence and enjoyment when reading.

Ready for a Level 2 (Beginning to Read) book

A child should:

- be able to recognize a bank of common words quickly and be able to blend sounds together to make some words.
- be familiar with using beginner letter sounds and context clues to figure out unfamiliar words.
- sometimes correct his/her reading if it doesn't look right or make sense.
- be aware of the need for a slight pause at commas and a longer one at periods.

A valuable and shared reading experience

For many children, reading requires much effort, but adult participation can make reading both fun and easier. Here are a few tips on how to use this book with a young reader:

Check out the contents together:

- read about the book on the back cover and talk about the contents page to help heighten interest and expectation.
- discuss new or difficult words.
- chat about labels, annotations, and pictures.

Support the reader:

- give the book to the young reader to turn the pages.
- where necessary, encourage longer words to be broken ... syllables, sound out each one, and then flow the syllables together; ask him/her to reread the sentence to check the meaning.
- encourage the reader to vary her/his voice as she/he reads; demonstrate how to do this if helpful.

Talk at the end of each book, or after every few pages:

- ask questions about the text and the meaning of the words used—this helps develop comprehension skills.
- read the quiz at the end of the book and encourage the reader to answer the questions, if necessary, by turning back to the relevant pages to find the answers.

Series consultant, Dr. Linda Gambrell, Distinguished Professor of Education at Clemson University, has served as President of the National Reading Conference, the College Reading Association, and the International Reading Association.

Senior Editor Victoria Taylor
Designer Sandra Perry
Senior Designer Anna Formanek,
David McDonald
Design Manager Nathan Martin
Managing Editor Laura Gilbert
Publishing Manager Julie Ferris
Publishing Director Simon Beecroft
Pre-production Producer Rebecca Fallowfield
Producer Melanie Mikellides
Jacket Designer Jon Hall

Reading Consultant
Dr. Linda Gambrell PhD.

First American Edition, 2013
Published in the United States by DK Publishing
345 Hudson Street, New York, New York 10014
DK, a Division of Penguin Random House LLC

Page design copyright © 2018 Dorling Kindersley Limited

18 19 20 10 9 8 7 6 5 4 3 2
014 – 187447 – Feb/13

DK books are available at special discounts when purchased in bulk
for sales promotions, premiums, fund-raising, or educational use.
For details, contact: DK Publishing Special Markets, 345 Hudson
Street, New York, New York 10014   SpecialSales@dk.com

A catalog record for this book is available
from the Library of Congress.

ISBN: 978-1-4654-0176-2 (Paperback)
ISBN: 978-1-4654-0177-9 (Hardcover)

Printed and bound in China

A WORLD OF IDEAS:
SEE ALL THERE IS TO KNOW

www.dk.com
www.starwars.com
www.LEGO.com/starwars

Contents

SUPER-VILLAINS

Written by Victoria Taylor

Batman   Robin

The Heroes

The world's super heroes have got a lot of work to do. They must keep the crime-filled streets of Gotham City and Metropolis safe.

There is a frightening group of super-villains causing havoc! They enjoy making things as difficult as possible for the super heroes.

Wonder Woman

Superman

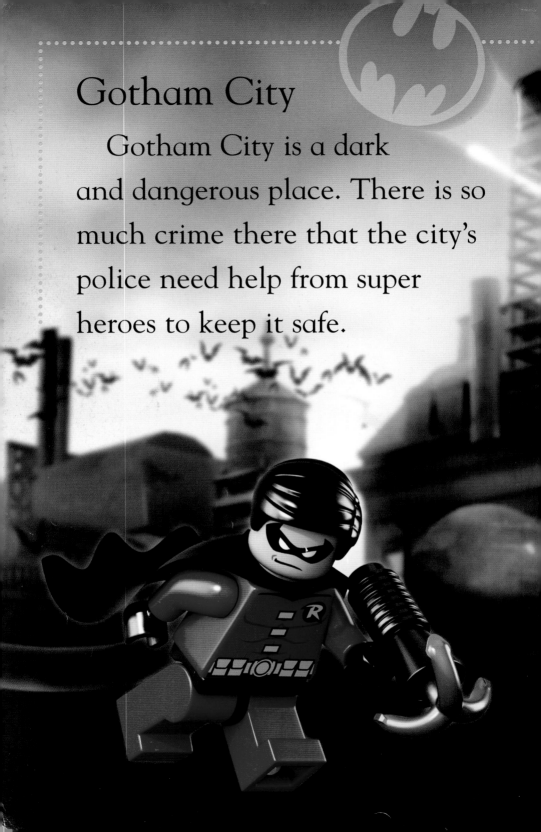

Gotham City

Gotham City is a dark
and dangerous place. There is so
much crime there that the city's
police need help from super
heroes to keep it safe.

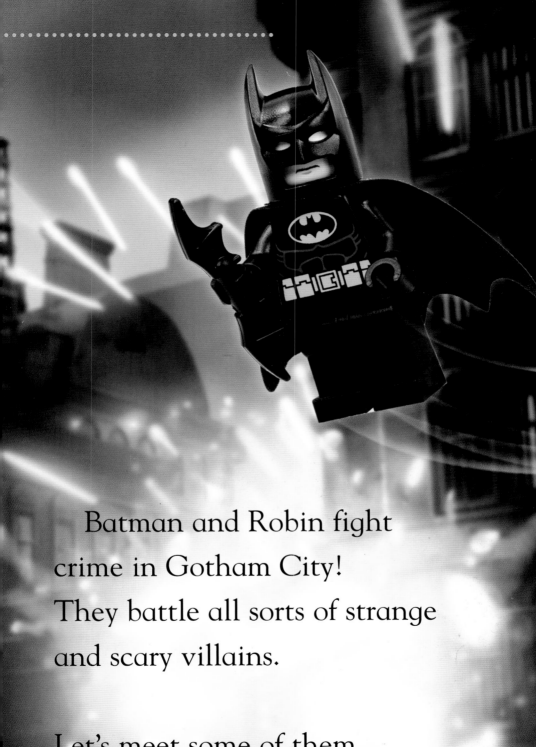

Batman and Robin fight
crime in Gotham City!
They battle all sorts of strange
and scary villains.

Let's meet some of them . . .

The Joker

The Joker is one villain that Batman does not find funny! He has a white face, bright green hair, and a permanent smile.

The Joker does not take being bad too seriously. He has all kinds of joke-themed weapons and gadgets.

He loves to surprise Batman whenever he can. Bang!

Mr. Freeze

Mr. Freeze enjoys doing battle on ice!

He likes cold, snowy conditions that match his frosty personality.

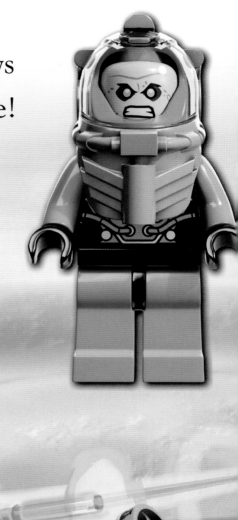

He can turn his enemies into
blocks of ice with a freeze pistol
that freezes them on the spot.

Luckily, Batman is too
fast for him!

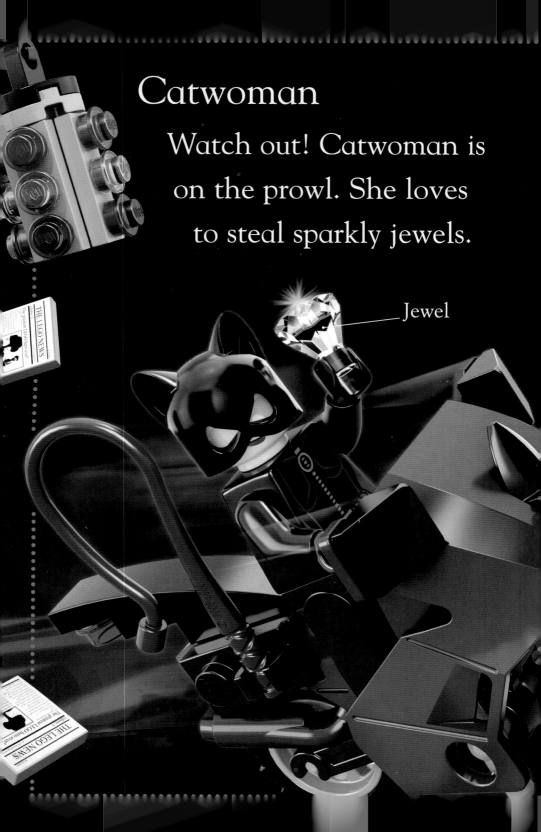

Catwoman

Watch out! Catwoman is
on the prowl. She loves
to steal sparkly jewels.

Jewel

Catwoman can climb tall buildings with ease. She wears a black suit that helps her hide from Batman and blend into the night.

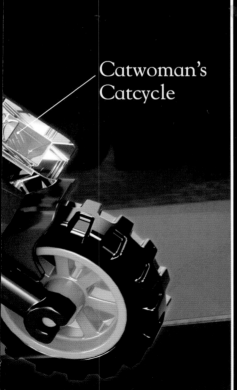

Catwoman's Catcycle

Well-protected

Catwoman carries a whip and wears a mask to hide her identity when stealing jewels.

Harley Quinn

Harley Quinn used to be
a doctor at Arkham Asylum.
She once treated the Joker there.

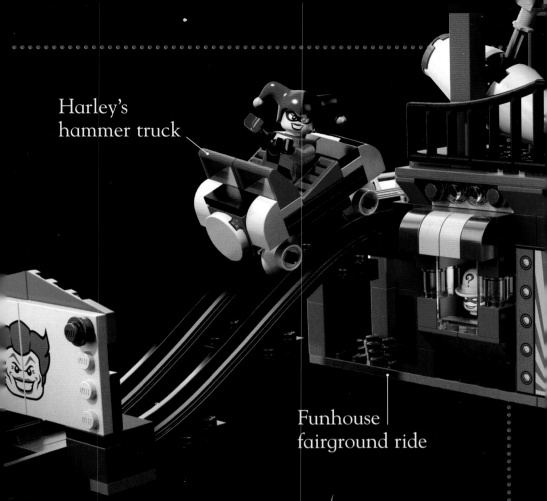

Harley's
hammer truck

Funhouse
fairground ride

But Harley ended up
forming a criminal duo with
the Joker instead of curing him
of his madness! The two villains
are on a joint mission to defeat
Batman once and for all.

Two-Face

Two-Face is double trouble.
He was in an accident that
turned him into the terrifying
villain Two-Face.
He is a master bank robber.

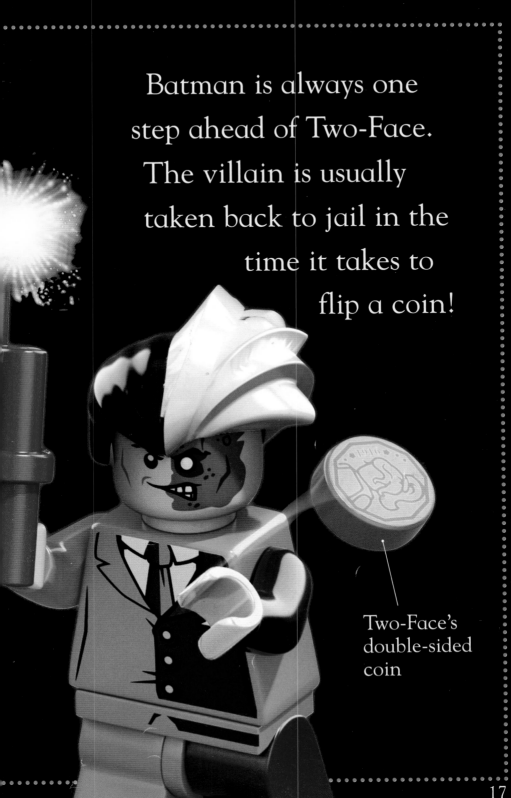

Batman is always one
step ahead of Two-Face.
The villain is usually
taken back to jail in the
time it takes to
flip a coin!

Two-Face's
double-sided
coin

Scarecrow

Scarecrow looks terrifying with his glowing red eyes. He wears ragged clothes and loves to scare people.

He flies an old-fashioned biplane, which has four wings.

He might look horrific, but Batman isn't scared of him!

Bane's Tumbler

Bane

Bane is one of the Batman's toughest enemies. He is very strong. He is also very clever and is good at planning his crimes in great detail.

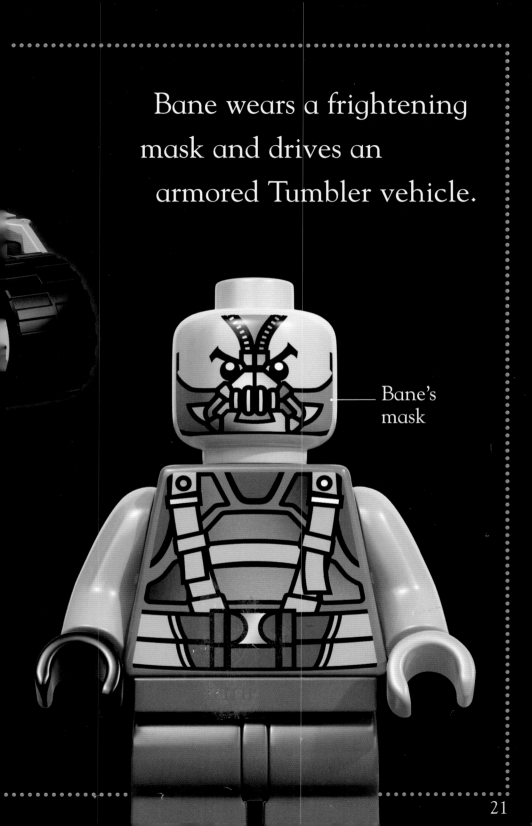

Bane wears a frightening mask and drives an armored Tumbler vehicle.

Bane's mask

The Riddler

Can you guess who this is?
It's the Riddler! He loves puzzles
and word games.
He even carries
a cane in the
shape of a
question mark!

Green suit

Question
mark belt

The Riddler always leaves
lots of clues about his crimes.
He loves watching Batman
struggle to solve his puzzles
and riddles.

Poison Ivy

Poison Ivy is one of Batman's most dangerous foes. She has always liked plants more than people.

Poison Ivy uses plant toxins to control the minds of others. She wears a costume made of leaves.

Vine

Poison Ivy has a whip made from a vine. She wants Gotham City to become overrun with wicked weeds.

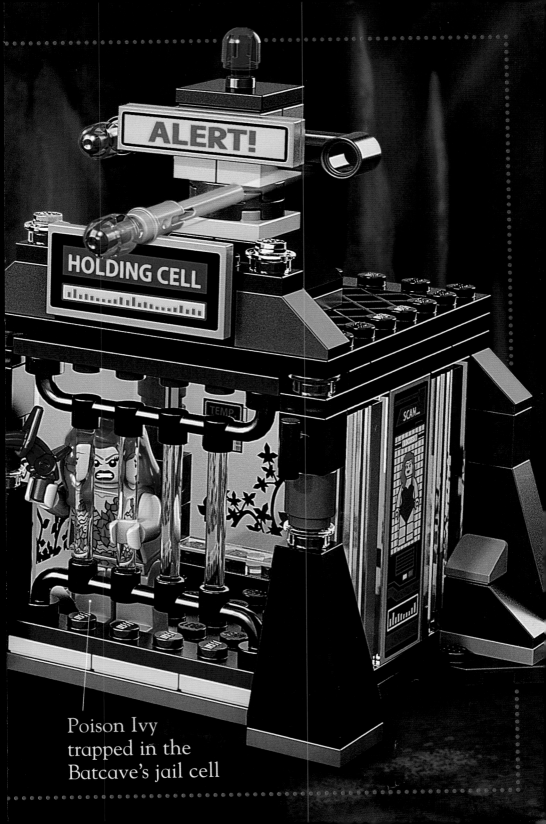

Poison Ivy
trapped in the
Batcave's jail cell

Metropolis

Batman and Robin have got Gotham City covered. Metropolis also has super hero protection against criminals and villains—Superman!

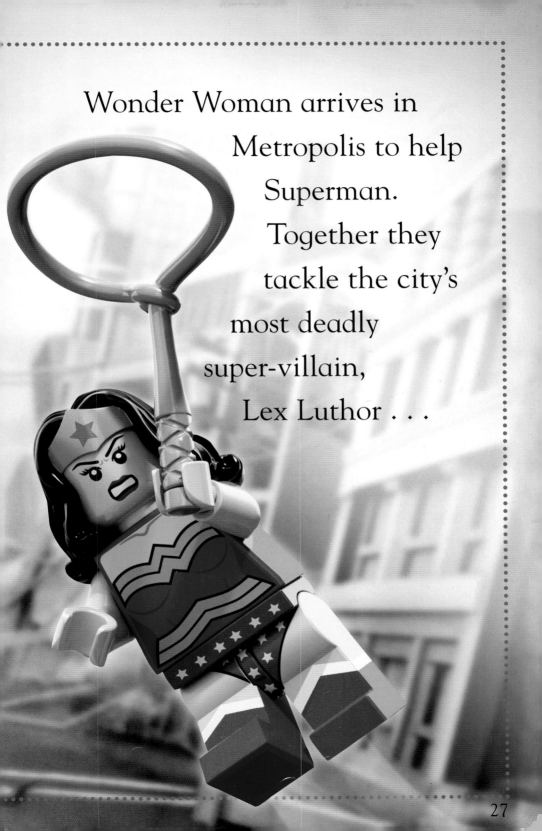

Wonder Woman arrives in Metropolis to help Superman. Together they tackle the city's most deadly super-villain, Lex Luthor . . .

Lex Luthor

Lex Luthor has been Superman's enemy for a long time. Bald baddie Lex is a rich businessman and inventor.

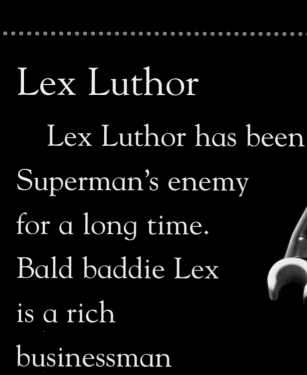

Lex's robot invention

Kryptonite gun
Lex invented a gun that is powered by Kryptonite. Superman becomes weak when faced with Kryptonite.

Lex loves to create his own weapons and equipment to help him to defeat Superman.

He has even invented a big robot that he can sit inside and control. It is super-strong but it is no match for Superman and Wonder Woman. He will have to invent something else!

Locked Up

The planet's super-villains have many different powers and tricks up their sleeves. However, in the end they are no match for the super heroes!

The villains end up behind bars for their crimes.

Well done, super heroes!

Quiz

1. Whose weapon is this?

2. What is Catwoman's vehicle called?

3. What is this villain called?

4. Whose biplane is this?